SO-EIA-780

GUNSIGHT

GUNSIGHT

THEODORE WEISS

New York University Press 1962

Publication of this work was made possible by

a partial subsidy from THE FORD FOUNDATION,

to whom the publishers make grateful

acknowledgment.

GUNSIGHT

Squinting after morning, like a sentry
on a mountain top, you lie. The hospital
sheets bank round you, drifted as your sleep.
And midnight, come and gone, ghostly in swaddling
snow remains. You wait who would be one
with the flowerbed, stretched out in the court
below, one with your leg, a frozen block;
not rank like summer, bundled in that vase,
the roses choking in the oppressiveness
of their own breath.
                    By such route morning comes?
Now lies, flight fettered in the ice, wedged
against the pane, as though a pulse throbbed there.
And somewhere, hiding a few stubbed wings, your Robin-
Hooded Wood, leaves fallen like the fairy
tales you stormed through, fumbles in the wind
for berries, fuzzy low faces you once picked,
oozing from your fingertips.
                    Yet lie here
stony as you will, time, unabated, whirls,
its stars more wily than the dark's snowflakes,
inside your flesh.
                    Even as you drowse
the corridor starts up its echoing.
Morning blue-lipped on her rattling tray,
she, white-breast, black-capped, -winged and -clawed,

arrives. That gimlet look, how far it's come,
like something out of snow. Bent over you,
snow peering into snow, arch, starched,
stiffest nun she is.
                              Quiet, she says.
Quiet to heal this feverishness? Scraps
of peace, placid nights, best baiting, rouse it,
greedier as it feeds.
                                   Now let them hack it
out, the mouth clamped fast in you; and then,
no longer hobbled to this leg, you shall walk
forth erect and free again or else
let death prevail . . .

                                        needle plunged,
the room begins to rock.
                                   A January
hillock knees, unblinking snow claws up.
Down corridor's funnel on a swooping knuckled
cloud, the suck and buffet of the sea.
Doors worked by whisper's hissing draft
swivel you to a crackling wilderness
of lights,
                    explosive glare a gash of knives,
one vast black-lacquered eye.
                                        Snowy masks

bent over you,
          voices flaking,
                 falling,

falling
       through the seasick smell

             breathe in

let me go, it's cold.

         Faces, walls
fling up at you, cavernous waves, snow-kneading
hands.

      Oh fie, that smell

          breathe in

             deep
past breathing, stench of bodies rotting.
              Distance,
many-hooded, sidles in. A mountain
stoops.

      How far it's come!

Through the crack shapes,
muffled, flickering,

can't breathe!

For crying
out loud, cut the shaking. Want to wake
the whole damn wood?

This jabbing cold,

a bunch
of voices, billowy up and down the air,
prickles everywhere.

It's only sticky
cobwebs, twigs. You got the gun. Thought
you said you wanted to hunt?

Something, skittering,
flaps against your mouth.

The dawn wind blowing
up—will you look at that lake skidaddle!

Let's go back.

Old scaredy cat, scrounge down;
keep your eye on that crack where midnight's roosting.

There in the trees like morning, dew on them,

sparrows, by the trillions, squabbling,

the dew's own shrillness,

       and a giant one,

the sun,

   see that in its beak?

      Wings spout.

Now's the time. Charge!

     Summer pitching
in its leaves, the wood a wilderness of lights,
of one bird zooming through another's flight,

what are you waiting for? Shoot! Shoot!

bullets ricochet—the flock like hurtling
stones—against each rock, each tree.
                                                East,
west, the breaking lake, its waters lashed
to wings, all, echoing, roar.
                                        Across the gunset
heavens redbreast day is
                                falling,
                                        flushed
and falling,
                body through which morning sang.

Only a handful, take it.

                    It's still warm

(come, my love, and lie with me)

still struggling in my hands

                                you wanted it,
now it's all yours.

                    July storming the mouth

can't breathe

(we'll lip to lip in mastery
enlarge the airs our senses sing,
the hanging gardens fingers bring)

and through the heart the heartless sea, oozings
from the fingertips,
                                that eye, that black
and glaring eye,

                        won't close.

                                Don't throw it away.
You musn't use the gun for that!

                                        Still

it stares.

                Where you going?

                                Feathers twirling,

        tumbled
                over drifts

                        (the hills and valleys
hovering, the seas of love)

down slippery peaks

                    to their blooming summit **time** . . .

lolled on a herd-browsed cloud of clover,

                         Laura!

Inside this spinning bed we rove,
delve into each treasure-trove.

From her hands and mouth it swells.

                         In coil-
ing warmth we lie that love, untoil-
ing, forage in us, finding, share
its raptures in our blended air.

Exultant, love, the looter, slams its waves
through you.

            Our honey-suckled kiss
plucking us, we blithely crest
the tide; like a sprig in the beak
of a dove we, soaring, wake

to fall head over heels

                    into the clover

closing round.

                Roses ring us, sweet sighs
mixed with ours.

                Roses by a field,
choking on their breath and on the piled
manure:
            the wrangling smells, the groans, the rattled
gaspings on the ground,
                    her hair alive,
hissing, twisting, rush of wings,

                    that glaring
rigid through your eyes!

                  The trees loop over,
tangled limbs, lips, cries . . .

                    reeling,
caterwauling,

don't leave me,

                    night hauling
them to rocky port, the sailors weave
you in as they are woven round with heaving
breasts and rouge-fixed faces,

                        Birdie, Gertie,

Madge and Meg,

             making light of mid-
night stark,
         mouths like wounds,

                   she wiggles, hot stuff,
sizzling on a spit,

           sinuous smoke,
twigged and shagged with ice, hands looking after,
horror in such white hands;
               and slyly winking
from your polished shoes as on the needle
in and out the olive-drab, crookback
of the journey, tracked through cloth like thread;
its knotting torments.

O I'll tear loose . . .

swept out to shallow cheering, reef of faces,
Mother weeping, Father coughing up
a smog, preacher, teacher, reef of faces,
foamy with questions

(say, how many feathers
on a ruffled breast?
its songs, its load
of flights, where do they rest?)

Shore recoils,
dawn shipwrecked in the toppling clouds, the breakers
of a handkerchief, the cry spun out
into the heave and tumble of the sea.

The black ship, drenched with slops, tosses round
in sleep that mumbles, tide-like, over them;
the sea itself gliding, ghostly dreams,
below, a thousand men smuggle the spoils
of continents,

souvenirs brought home
for Birdie, Madge and Meg,

Lügers clicking;
helmets; like a lidless eye the ruby
Joe hacked off a finger for; and tight-
packed voices, babbling lucid as these waves,

snug in our packs with brush and comb, tooth
by jowl with Gertie snapt, the spicy note,

they try to read between the scribbled lines
as in the sea,
                    time billows to white unbroken,
daze like drifting mountainous snow . . .

                                        after weeks
of olive-drab waiting:
                    dumped in a crummy town,
cards from some ancient game, the crumpled dreams,
the tattered jokes, the hands stuck like a clock's.

Over the barracks sparrows flying, flying,
sun reaped in their wings as in the trumpets
and percussives of the tootling band.

And by the drill shed, never breaking ranks,

soldiers, fall in; count off; now cock your rifles,
aim and . . .

       flocks on flocks, dragging the world
away, a great wind blowing up behind.

Round and round the company, shuffling, goes
a million miles in one small khaki circle
while dance—the ragged gods you once in long-
gone youth befriended—fumbles after limbs,
the pin-up slumped to rutted eyes,

                come on,
boy, it don't mean a thing
if you aint got that swing,

         the legs cast up
and away in the jig of war, the reedy piper,
death, blows through the lusts, the memories,
you and the rest lice sizzling on a leaf
in the wind's lull,

       aw, I'm stuffed to the gizzard
with shave, shit and shinola. We got the pass,
let's make the most of it. A roll in the grass,

that's what I'm for, the water far below
a bare-assed shimmy

                    (*we crest the tide,*
high on a jaunty world-wide
spring in a bird's beak)

                              sweeping back and forth,
billowy heat . . .

                    two-bit sweating Anacapri,
a morning long, a leaf. Sun sashays in
and popples razzle-dazz under its feet,
grapes, plums and dames panting to be plucked.
This is where July shacks up.

                         The town,
dangling from its mountain slope, a fleece,

it's a sheep's life all right, stinks like a goat;
but you got to admit the flock, flooding
down the hill, is flashing in the sun,

its backside in a clump of olives, teeters
on three lopsided streets,

wash smacking out—
and what a sail, a whale, a zepplin maybe—
the baggy drawers of Poppa Zookie. His cheeks
popt with grins like fish flopping in
a net, the town, its kids and dogs, yipping
at his heels, he grabs us with his smoochy kisses.

And down below, splashing up,

                    the fat-assed

washerwomen,

        blue-backed, sun-whacked waves.

Smack them as you drink this vino, singing
O Sole Mio, sun blinking boozy through.

Spring it was at first, a morning long,
a leaf. Now summer gluts, July hunched down,
relentless with its whorish herd of never-
closing blooms, its gasping days, the sunlight
raspy with the muck it's lapping, turning
into dust.
        Dust everywhere: those old men,
squatting by the cemetery wall,
the world, its past, dead weight upon their backs,

like ghosts wheeze up their ancestors.

Poor coot,

can't tell your great-grandfather from a gnu.
Go digging down inside your dust, one poke
you're through.

      The pebbles crunching underfoot
are bones; in moldy crusts, in cheese each munches
on the dead, wine gurgling down the throat
their guttural blood.

      Your town's a smoky coal-
and-iron dump; day and night it vomits
crap and noise on everything. In these
old boys still many a jig is kicking up,
like dancing-girls from centuries ago,
twisting through the dirt.

      Twisted
bits of women, broken from the start,
these ancient wraiths, heads bent together, sigh—
black shawls like shrouds—through fingers, bony needles
in the middle of their webs.
      Their keening
and that steady low-down roar, the hordes

complaining in a too small bed, a voice
more nettling than war.

Grab the jug.
A couple more steps up the hill and, there,
you're out of it. The wine, the babes, that's
the spring to dive into.

The knoll waiting,
knees bent for an outing, the war folded
away in the light, a dog-eared history book
to prop the table, folded away like paper
ruins, the calendar of shattered days
and nights ript out, of scattered cities dropt,
the countless lives . . .

the nine lined up,

the dunces,
faces to the board at the teacher's order,

teacher's orders, days remote, humdrum
as school,

secure as home, no bug snugger
in its grassy summer,

home? its stances
and pretences . . .

your Father can sit still,
hours on the stoop carving a peg-leg
for that chick. But does he think of us?

Father, Father, where are you?

That's the boat
I promised you. Take this paper, fold it
here and here, it's ready to be launched
to dare whatever waves the Creek can blow.

(Listen to your Mother; don't go near the water)

Puff a mouthful, off it scoots.
(Phew!
A cargo of your Father's pheasants, pigeons,
cuckoo Noah's ark)

Trust it, Son;
speedier than any line you draw,
McCreedy's Creek whips you into the Bay
of Biscay, Venice, and the open sea

*where the West Indies dance like spicy leaves
upon a tree.*

Frank, where are you steering us?

*That bobbing isle's the hideout for the likes
of me, old Captain Kidd himself.*
                                    But first

we got to shoot

            *(soldiers, line them up;
cock your rifles, aim. No time, supplies,
for prisoners . . .*
                the nine . . .
                            the dunces, faces
to the wall . . .)

                bang, bang, bang

                            (tangled
limbs, lips, cries . . .)

                shove them off
*the deck and hurry up; the shore, the morning's
just a step.*
                Jump!

It's too rocky
to land, too deep and dark.

You got the bird,
a gold leaf in its beak, to wing you to that
sacred spot: treasure, sunsets, battles,
buried where a limb sticks out and midnight
always roosts.
My wooden leg'll stamp;
earth rattles and they pop.

(Watch it! Pigface
Sarge
old Pontius Preacher
Teacher
is bearing
down on you . . .)

Teacher scrawls a curve
upon the board and, Columbus gayly bobbing,
it is Spain, refuge of the dawn,
its winter gardens blossoming;
another
wriggling stroke

like Pocahontas Susie's
pigtails, black and snaky, and her shaky
two-way jiggle as her garter, smacking,
sends you, sends.

        Now snap it.

                    Something's breaking

loose!

    (only a flock of quail, Son,
winter white-hot, nipping, at their tails)

The world whips by like smoke and crumpled papers
from a train, scraps of cities, distance,
stuck to it, the crazy seasons wrangling.

And your country, spooky in the sun
with highways: miles and miles of no one, nowhere,

better stay where you belong, Son, holding
on to what's your own,

                  secure as home,
humdrum as school! That's not the rule you learned.
Even as you pledge allegiance

to trickery

in the cloakroom

whatever's clutched soon snatches
out of hand.

A face looms over us?

Out of dirty books and bodies—lice sizzling
on a leaf in a wind's lull—the Facts,
acrid with their beetling look, the chalk

who dared to scribble that nasty word across
the board?

sour old teacher stinks, ink
and droning voices, sex and summer hum,
as through the barred-off window you are brightest
scholar of, remote in daylight swarming,
Gooseberry Hill lifts its violet text,
then tips, like birds wing-propt, rippling twilight—

Susie's eyes that wink at what she's thinking—

and into the woods it dives of crow-quilled words,
dumb now like dizzy numbers rubbed off the board,

erasers beating, puffed into a cloud
of chalk, into the dark and into the stars
as valentines are cheating in the desk.

There in the empty cloakroom the Milkman's Son

I'm an old cowhand

               is skillfully working over
the pearl-and-ruby, eighteen-carat movements
of the Jeweler's well-set Daughter.

                    Get her
in a corner: you got a hell of a lot
of catching up to do.

                (In one second
I will teach you more than ten Dogfaces
can in a million books and a trillion years.)

Use this map, the pieces like a jigsaw
fit. That's the clue. You're getting hot.
The answer, treasure, 's at the end of that.

       It's Love, LOVE, L O V E makes the world go **round.**
       Get into the spin, boy, be jet-propelled.
       Here are the curves, boy, from which to spill.

Here are the swerves, quick trip to the moon.
He who won't take it 's an ass-faced baboon.
So come on, boy, kick your feet off the ground.
*It's Love, LOVE, L O V E makes the world go **round.***

Her garter, snapping, starts a swell that rams
the air—a gap in nature—people popping.
Smoke and snowflakes craze the sky. An engine
batters on the tracks, its lonely nightmare
whistle shrieking, moaning. Midnight slouches
down the street.

                 (Or is it morning, stiff
and glazed,
        the crack,
            the narrow crack,
                    where day
and darkness meet?)

          The recess crams with yelling
Polish kids.

       PHEEEEEEEEEUW! There he goes

         Momma's boy, Momma's boy,
         pants like a hog,
         grunts like a frog,
         can't turn round cause
         he's stuck like a bog.

Mid-winter
dark, a thousand corners crouching, keeping
terror bright, a genius, it, coiling,
leaps.
    Run!

        Scaredy cat, scaredy cat . . .

                the cold

deep past breathing

          is ripping through.
                Slopes
sliding under you,
        you stumble,
              fall,
                roll
like a snowman
       round and round
            through drifts
to their blooming
       summit time.
            Everywhere
a peak frosting your roof, snow-lapped, earth-

hugged, leaf-snug berries, tangy through, the oozing
fingers of Gooseberry Hill . . .

O.K.,
boy, grab that bucket and let's go.
Susie, you come too. We'll pick the big
fat berries on the way.

**I can't get through
these prickly bushes, over these rocks,**

these rocks
and rills, round templed hills: high time you learned
a thing or two.
Now both hunch down. Clutch
the hillside, kid; you're Jack in the Beanstalk.
And by the maple, trying out the seasons,
sweaty summer red-faced at the fence,
when you reach the hilltop

it's muddy here,

and Mother

(listen to your Father: you
can trust it; be a man, Son)

your turn's next.
I'll warm things up. While we plan out maneuvers
in the barn, you play soldier.
And like a sentinel stuck to his post
keep yours; anyone who sleeps or runs away
is traitor and must die

> *(must die and die*

and die)

> *if someone comes you know the signal*

her garter smacks

> *(count off, cock your rifles:*
get ready, get set)

> *march*

> *then we drill*
and drill till trees salute and birds—the redcoats
are coming, beware, beware!—stand at attention
mid-air

> see that white inside the door,
that gasping through the straw, the tickled cry?

Those hands reaching out,

        horror in such white hands!

(twigs and sticky cobwebs . . .)

        come on, scaredy
cat, now's your chance. I fixed it . . .

        (charge!)

FEE, FIE, FO, FUM,

        the signal,

thrashing in the strawy dark?

        I SMELL

Oh fie, fie!

        THE RUTTED SWEAT, THE BLOOD

Father!

        What's eating you? You got away.

It's only your own tracks hotfooting after.
Now, still oozing bloody from your finger-
tips, the batch of berries that you picked,
jam them in a jar, baptise with spit.

Right behind their fuzzy low faces who's that
pushing through the bushes?

> (*a scarecrow*)

                             shapes
like men of crusted snow, numbers slipping
from the night's blackboard

                (*a rash of stars*
marching up Gooseberry Hill)

                   the Polack kids

(*the nine, nameless, faceless, lined up*)

                        snarling
charge.
      Your lunchbox clattering on stone,
they corner you, pinned to the schoolyard wall.
Terror, lean, a genius, croons, the world

one giant wintry glare.
>   Give them your apple,
sandwiches,
>   the cake.

>   Still they come.
I've nothing more.

>   There's more to you than that:
stumbling up the hill, throw them your gloves,
and then your hat, your coat . . .

>   *get him,*
>   *fat little four-eyes,*
>   *teacher's pet,*
>   *momma's tit,*
>   *poppa's snot,*
>   *one cent the lot,*
>   *get him!*

A shot rings out; the wood a sortie of dark,
trees loop over

>   *hunch down and hug*

>   *(we all know*
what you two are doing in the dark . . .)

faces, passion-twisted, flicker down
the street.
        Behind them, sprawled like crackling bugs
fallen from the corner lamp, the millhands
on their porches grunt.
        Belching fumes,
dumped over their lumpy wives, they roar along
the chutes; through the molten heart of the mill
faces heap

      which way did the little bastard
go?
  Get him, get him!

      Figures, hurtling,
ricochet, cries of fire,

      Father,
where are you?

      engines stutter, crashing
iron cars,
    the sputtering shells crush over

an openness:
    light on light is breaking

through . . .

        just one step more we reach the top.
There we can picnic, watch the whole damn world
go by.
     Hey, soldier, look. Behind that tree,
waving a stick, the scarecrow's come alive.
He's scooting up the hill. After him!

Guns glint, the world slashing like sun on water,
faces flaring,
        plunging,

           he's turning. Shoot,
shoot I tell you while you can.
                Atta boy,
you winged him good.
           He's falling.
                 Wait for me!

His black eyes shadowing, his arms outstretched,
he's clawing through the air, into the dirt,

horror in such white hands,

        the rutted sweat,

the blood, words spluttering, caught by that endless
moment, helpless waiting, face to face:
July clogged, hunching over both of you,
a glitter as of snows mixed in with summer;

far below, the same light striking fire
from the waves, the black-shawled, wintry shapes,
bent at the town's one well, beat their clothes.

Snow blinkless in his eyes

                       (the glaring rigid

through your eyes)

                  the lightning on the stock,
the morning, focused wholly on you, lock:
the vast unblinking icy look,

                       watch out

for his gun!

          the lightning on . . .

                    can't see,

I'll smash it,

don't use your gun for that.
All spies got to be taken prisoner.

No time, supplies,
                    the cake,
                              the hat,
                                       the lies.

Strike it, crush that glaring eye forever:
the blow,
          again
               and again
                         and again . . .

how many men you trying to kill?

                                   A shot
rings out, a sortie of dark,

                         (*hunch down and hug . . .*)

crashing iron cars, sputtering shells,
a thousand clashing knives, burst round,

                                        my leg!

into the dirt, the groans, the rattled gaspings
as you writhe.

Frank, Frank, help me!

For Christ sake, got to get you out of here.
Throw your arms round my neck,
not so tight . . .

down through roots and rocks,
a hornet's seething
mill,

what's this beaked thing over me?
It stares ecstatic. Oh the black lake's stuck.

Across the gunset heavens, redbreast day,
flushed and dripping, feeds a pulpy weed

(the roses by us, sweet and . . .)

choking smell.

A body lurches, cold, stiff, flight fettered
in the air as though a pulse throbbed there;

from some far mountain spring, a common source,
the drops, coursed through your eyes, mouth, breath,
collect.

How cross this great divide?

It's only
the narrow crack where day and darkness meet.
Grab the bird and stamp;
                    and as the earth
begins to rattle,
                jump . . .

                        cavernous waves,
the heave and tumbling sea . . .

                            here's the boat
I promised you . . .

                east, west, the ship
is tossing; billows clamber summits over you.
The ship is hoisting

            skull-&-bones!

                    And those

that smiled—

      butcher, baker, teacher, preacher,
undertaker—

      swarthy faces, snarling
at the rail.

      There's nothing you can trust . . .

that bird, its gold leaf lighting up the way . . .

You zigzag like a furled-out, wind-flopt moth.
The breakers, toppled, hurl you onto roaring
rocks.
      The stooping, ice-capt mountain shatters;
upright from its evil-smelling cleft
figures flit like smoke shot from your breath,
straining for blood to cross the fuming gap.

Darkness belches round,
                a wild-eyed scream,

how dare you come below?

            The nine, shapeless,

nameless, charge:
                    forms like clawing dreams,

no, no, you must not drink, not you, not you . . .
your face, twisted, shifting with every look,
don't make me see it!

                    Having chosen this,
you have no other choice; you have . . .

each wiping out the last about to speak . . .
Frank, how have you, a wound for mouth, sped here?

Not by what the flesh can do; your breath
North Wind enough, swifter than your black ship,
I, timely as the rites of spring, arrive.

While I trudge these many cumbered months
through body's dead-of-winter?

                    Through body's cold
and dead you build your winter.

                              Lament is nearing;
swollen cataract, weeping wails . . .
                    my name!

The waters, surging, mouth me.

                        Flesh gives,

                                    white-

capt voices,

            the Shrouded Ones.

                        Something sucks

(forgetting boasts them all!)

                        each act, each thought.

Expect to keep that churning pulse, the dark's
and time's, their rancorous secrets, hid forever?

You its one supply of breath, the crop springs:
woman gabble, dreams orgy-fleshed, the dead,
recent and old, fierce by their former fairness.

Mother, why do you, pale as hoar-frost glimmer-
ing on leaves, my blood upon your lips,
appear?

Well you may ask. Not even here
do you embrace me first. Your blood you call it.
Long before your birth your stranger heart
wrenching itself from mine, how admit

my cry in every drop?

> *Yet rightly your question*
belongs to me. The pain you gave above
sufficed. I stopped. I am here now because
I wish—no less than have—to be.

Help me,

Mother.

> *Those outstretched hands are hardly meant*
for me. Dead I am and, as you are,
dead to you. Much better so than waking
old torment.
> > *But why do you want two deaths?*
One satisfies most. Still it is not surprising.
The dark haunts you and you desire it
as I could not throw off my bitter longing.

Even here I counted days, pushed them by
in hope of you. My hunger, like these tears,
real in a shadow's eyes, groping, goes on.
And shall until you feed it in yourself.

Why do you who would never let me go —
talk to this fever, Mother,

but now no mistake
of shielding can be made—by your own blood,
first drunk of me, I tell you—against the trials
you have to go through still,

tell this aching
a story as you used to, make it let me
go — why do you avoid me now?

Try hard
as you will you cannot touch me, any more
than I, striving all my life, touched you.

Farewell, farewell. Much as mist can wish,
I, once your mother, wish you, still my son.
When, the last time, I hold forth my hand
again, you will indeed be much embraced
and, so gathered, ever stay in me.

Oh stay . . .
but who are these following you?

A mow of women, faces flashing, most
naked of their names as of their flesh.
Not only those you know but glamors of time

your mind cohabits with, imagination's
grossness. Mainly those who, trusting, gave
themselves to you.
                    And do: as flakes they come,
your breath the blast that whirls them round as once
it failed them in its falterings.
                    And come,
now through your will working their own, fierce
by their former fairness.
                    Last and fairest,

                                        Laura,

driving them! O why do you, your body
like a new moon blazing through these clouds
it chars, lour at me?

            Never
can I forget that moment's forgetting;
see, it boasts them all! This time
you shall not leave.

                    How bear that thrashing
in my hands? Tenderness, the very moment
it rose in me, drove terror near, the cold
ferocity that, nimbler than the morning,
climbed your eyes.

     Even as we lay there,
summer's aim, the roses and the lambs
become an ambush . . .
        don't go; don't forgive,
and so forget, me.
      Wind slipt through my fingers,
smoke in the gust of her own sighs, she melts.

But the others do not disdain to drink of me!

Who are you would batter your way down **here,**
and with your body on? No breaking bloody
bones, no tears of yours, can tide you through.

Faces flurry — fevers, buffets — against me.
You pale kingdoms glimmer as from a vault,
like cinders struck: my ancestors, all jostling,
peer.
   Not forgotten! The hacked and crushed,
as ashes recognizable, yet voices fleshed,
their gaze, their gestures fixed in speaking only.

Through the mist calls flicker:
        my youngest **dead,**
the few I began with, many days feted,
stuffed like hay-fat oxen, then struck down

by a single blow as one butchers at stall
for a wedding banquet;
                    through the gashes fumes:
rotting breath of festered years, youth wasted . . .

aether through the suffocating flowers,
high in this narrow room, banked on a cliff
of lilies, a waxen body lies;
                    the tangled
keening, birds beaked in my ears, the dead
weight aching in my hands . . .

                              birds, trillions of them,

and a giant one,

                    the sun,

                              through rushing trees
breaks loose

                    and so do I,

                              headlong as always . . .
Frank, wait for me.

                    You're the one won't wait.

Round and round you, chortling, leap. The moment
a scampering, rowdy hill, the sunlight sweeps
the boulders on both sides of us like beams
in its abounding will.
            But time won't wait,
the slender body thrashing in my hands,

that and the sly elated betrayals, sweet pain—

worlds and years between, what can I do? —

of helplessness . . .

                        sinewy moaning winds,
salt-mouthed as the sea, O do not snatch at me.

Striding like anger, a shooting-star, Father!
why do you refuse to look at me?
You're not dead?

        No more, no less than he
has always been to you, scared of the truth
he might have taught.

                    The openness: light

explodes. Help me!

Worlds and years and fears
between, what can he do?

He rams right through me.
Father, why don't you hear?

Get out your hacker,
whack the old bastard, cut down the beanstalk,
the golden pecker,
into the mouth and eyes,
that cry,

the body struggling, warm

(fumes
as from a slaughtered calf)

face gone out —
still it stares — that eye, that midnight-black
unblinking eye,
O all of them and all
these faces, clustered, jutting out, jeer
at me.
Break them, smash,

                    the lightning locks,
the world clots on the butt . . .

But the trajectory of that blow—how easy.
Fellow soldier, since you dare by act
and suffering to come this far, hear one
who knows and so can speak for all the dead.

Gone down into the harrowed, ice-gouged soil,
clods clutched in the ruts, the hammered looks
and screams, smeared on their mouths, in time crop
forth, grape- and lilac-fleshed.
                              Back now
with a naked truth the living are—even
with this hand clenching the sodden dogtag
round this neck—too sight-lashed for,
                                    like you,
the keeper.

             I? . . .
                    the blow, beating the face
together again and . . .
                         as I watch, a glitter
coils up, hissing, licking at my foot,

like something out of earth and out of snow,

you the keeper: father, mother, children
and their heirs—ghosts you must bear into life.

Oozings from my fingertips, all make,
heart's hammering,
                              the facets of one eye . . .
Father, Mother, Frank, the Shrouded Ones,
and . . .
                  you, the one I killed, barely covered,
green still in the earth, storming through
the others!

            Only by this many come:
through your efforts to avoid me home.
Shun as you will the violence in each thing,
most violently in hand and bird's bright-morning
song, do you think hiding long succeeds?

No treasure for us past what we have buried:
passions, loves rejected, banking up
their light and fire in the earth like restless
gems, the bird, the gutted morning, mouths.

Lie stony as you will, relentless time—
its stars more wily than the dark's snowflakes,
their fire needing to be fed—still whirls

and, unabated, will inside the flesh:
pain seeks you; doubt and anguish yearn.

O do not stare at me with such desire!
Shall the wronged, wrong itself, know love?
Please take this, drink with the rest and bless me
with forgetting. Let me go. Through the earth,
and into me, have you not burrowed enough?
It breaks me

       like the gun-struck thing I am.
Admire sores, black gaping gums, these sockets
filled with nothing.

               No, no! do not stoop
in this fanged light

         a wedding
banquet . . .
        picnic . . .
            fumy with manure . . .
it's roses, love
        (*it's Love,* LOVE, L O V E)

that frizzled grin, your eyes like owls, raking,
thrust a shiny darkness through me . . .

                                                out
to a clearing . . .
                        you, Father, Mother, blending,
bob, carcasses sizzling on one spit!

(*Love makes the world go round*)

                                        It's bending over,
stirring them . . .
                        I don't want to see it!
Don't they know I'm here?

                Love realises
nothing but itself, cares for nothing
but itself.

                The mouth, the wound, the beast
all tooth! . . .

                        who, hissing like wild fowl, a storm
of sickles bristling through my side, are you?

Tribes of tens-of-thousands your blood recalls.

Fie, ravage, crime, decay reek from your mouths.

Your frauds' familiars, those you sped by,
those who claim the life you long denied.
Try to escape? So ingrained are we in your glance,
its far end clotted with our hair, looking
away draws us nearer.
                                    Out of your breath,
crushed voices, trampled scenes, journeys waiting,
generations grating in one seed,
we burgeon now our summer's withheld might.

Where the end of terror? Fleeing the furies

hauls them into sight.

                              The beast at me,

the tooth!

          Through the length of your whole being
know it, feel it; then go, look after my life
and yours. That snaky head, a kindred too,
you must not yet confront. Nor swaddle in,
sipping the maggot's milk, homespun of spider.

Some things—the crag, the granite sea, the slug,
this mouth that grinds incessantly in you—
cannot be turned into the human. All

that we can do is try, while we are men,
to meet them humanly.
                    That time will come
when it must come, the time that does not seek
us out by name and does not recognize,
forgive or smile.
                Now I, having served,
return to earth that bore me of which I am —
in all these years of wandering and dread —
return. You too return, to these I leave,
the living isle, the human hour.
                            Where men
in cunning pass the avid fox, in skill
of greed exceed the swine, dawn also dwells;
still dawn tracks out her dancing-floor.
                                The night
involved, the Hunter on his knees, with terror
and catastrophe, see the great flocks
nestling in that song.
                    Remember me and these,
but locally, like lilac, bunched-out grapes,
and in conspirings of wind and sea.

Remember you? Nothing can be forgotten.
To be a living vault, inheritor
of all your griefs, spring brings flowers to

and summer chokes with plenty; to feel them thrusting
over me, the roses, flushed and puffy
with my breath.
                    Yet woods in every leaf
look away; even as I touch, in pools
blue-lipped water chars.
                    How can I push
this body to the top of my corruption-
crammed and -trammeled journey?
                              Look! The hillside,
rubbled cries in a rush, is tumbling down,
a green man, giant in his rise,

                    like something
out of snow,

              stalks reach out, July
bristling bayonets in shocks, a bellied
commerce, everywhere suckling a dead man's bones.

My name

              I never heard!

              multitudinous
in skittering leaves an autumn long, cicadas,

twisted sounds, in hail of skillful winds,
handling your black ship's shrouds.

                            By such gear morning
comes.
         Back now

               as the earth once pivoted
in your wrist

           into the motion, complex
music of the Pleiades, one with
Orion, rounding up his stately game,
the flock flooding down sky's terraces,
moonlit spoils he once pursued and fled,
herded like bees into the hiving dawn.

The ship's pitching, giving up one last
concerted cry,

           no less than men and beasts,
sky and the creature sea ride in its hold
as in that cry,

             slows to this bed.
                 Slobber
in every breath, through the hissing aether,

bit by bit, finger joined to finger,
the bird is gathering me.
                       I twirl in its beak,
a seed, a twig, burst at once into a wood,
the dawn perched askingly among its limbs.

Through the mist and through the hard scrutinous
light, thick flakes whirling, faces make
again.
       Soon, the window thawed, its frost
like mountain flowers strewn upon these day-
heaped sheets, the world, barefoot in my eyes,
as walking to and from my bed, once more
begins.